Sound

Written by Sally Hewitt

W

First published in 2009 by Franklin Watts
338 Euston Road, London NW1 3BH

Franklin Watts Australia
Level 17/207 Kent Street, Sydney NSW 2000

Editor: Katie Dicker
Art Direction: Dibakar Acharjee (Q2AMedia)
Designer: Neha Kaul (Q2AMedia)
Picture researcher: Kamal Kumar (Q2AMedia)
Craft models made by: Tarang Saggar (Q2AMedia)
Photography: Dibakar Acharjee (Q2AMedia)

Picture credits:
t=top b=bottom c=centre l=left r=right

Cover: Jupiterimages.
Title page: Doug Schneider/Istockphoto.
Insides: Getty Images: 6, Thaut Images/Fotolia: 7t,
Doug Schneider/IStockphoto: 7b,
BananaStock/Jupiterimages: 8t, Pathathai
Chungyam/Istockphoto: 8b, NASA: 10, David B
Fleetham/Photolibrary: 11, Caroline Clarke/Fotolia:
12b, Featurepics: 12t, Luislouro/Dreamstime: 14t,
Oguz Aral/Shutterstock: 14b, Eric Gevaert/Fotolia:
16t, Christopher Busch/Fotolia: 16b, Jane
Norton/Istockphoto: 18, Jupiterimages: 19t,
Masterfile: 20t, Alistair Heap/Alamy: 20b,
Marc Kozak/Istockphoto: 22, WizData, inc: 23t,
Chris Stock/Lebrecht/Photolibrary: 24,
Beth A. Keiser/Assosiated Press: 25t,
Creatas Images/Jupiterimages: 26, Michael A.
Keller/zefa/Corbis: 27t, Callalloo Canis/Fotolia: 27b.
Q2AMedia Image Bank: Imprint page, Contents page,
9, 11, 13, 15, 17, 19, 20, 21, 23, 25.

With thanks to our models Shruti Aggarwal and
Tarang Saggar.

A CIP catalogue record for this book
is available from the British Library

ISBN: 978 0 7496 8759 5

Dewey Classification: 534.'22

Printed in China

Franklin Watts is a division of Hachette Children's
Books, an Hachette UK company.
www.hachette.co.uk

Contents

Words that appear in **bold** can be found in the glossary on pages 28–29.

Sounds around us

The world we live in is full of sound – people talking, traffic roaring, birds singing and music playing. All these sounds give us information about what is going on around us.

Voices

Sounds help us to **communicate** with each other. We hear the sound of each other's voices when we talk. We hear our teacher at school giving us information and instructions and asking us questions.

We listen to the sound of a teacher talking to learn new things.

Danger!

Sounds warn us of danger. We listen for the sound of traffic before we cross the road. The school fire alarm warns us to get out of the building to safety. A fierce dog growls and warns us to keep away!

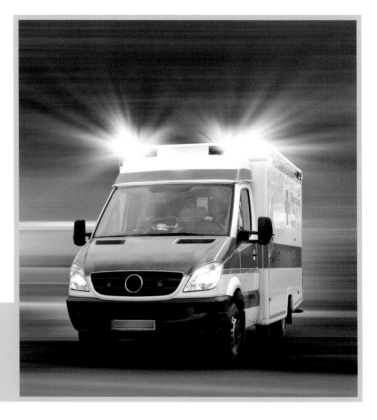

A loud siren warns us that an emergency vehicle is racing towards us.

Entertainment

Some sounds entertain us. We hear voices and sound effects on the radio, television, at the theatre and in the cinema. We enjoy listening to music and singing or playing a musical instrument to create sounds ourselves.

Earphones let us listen to music without disturbing other people.

Vibrations

Sounds are made when something moves and makes **vibrations**. These are very tiny movements to and fro that make **sound waves** in the air.

Moving

Big vibrations make loud sounds and small vibrations make quiet sounds. When you sit very still and whisper, you make quiet sounds because the air around you only vibrates a little. When you stamp your feet and shout, you make bigger vibrations.

At a playground, children make loud sounds by shouting and laughing.

When you sing, your vocal cords vibrate the air in your throat to make the sound of your voice.

Feeling sound

You can sometimes feel sound. If you put your hand on a radio playing loud music, you can feel the vibrations. Put your hand on your throat when you talk, laugh or sing, and you will feel your **vocal cords** vibrate.

Make a sound cannon

Ask an adult to help you with this activity

You will need:
- rectangle of strong card about 45 cm x 25 cm • extra card • sticky tape • felt tip pens • plastic from a sandwich bag • scissors
- square of tissue paper

1 Roll the card into a tube and tape it together to make a cannon. Decorate your cannon with felt tip pens. Stretch the plastic tightly over one end of the tube and tape it in place.

2 Cut out a card circle the same size as the end of the tube. Ask an adult to help you cut a small circle in the middle of it. Tape it over the open end of the tube.

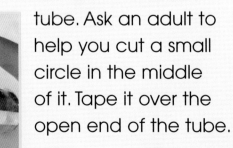

3 Cut one side of the tissue paper to make a fringe. Ask a friend to hold the tissue fringe in front of the hole in the cannon.

4 Tap the plastic at the other end of the cannon. Watch as the tap vibrates the air and makes sound waves that travel down the cannon and force air out of the hole, moving the tissue.

Moving sound

Sound needs to travel through something for us to hear it. When something moves, it makes vibrations which push against the **molecules** in **solids**, **liquids** and **gases** so they vibrate, too. This creates sound waves.

Silence

There is silence when sound has nothing to travel through. Silence means there is no sound. It is silent in space, for example, because there is no air in space for sound to travel through. In contrast, the Earth is surrounded by air that is full of sounds.

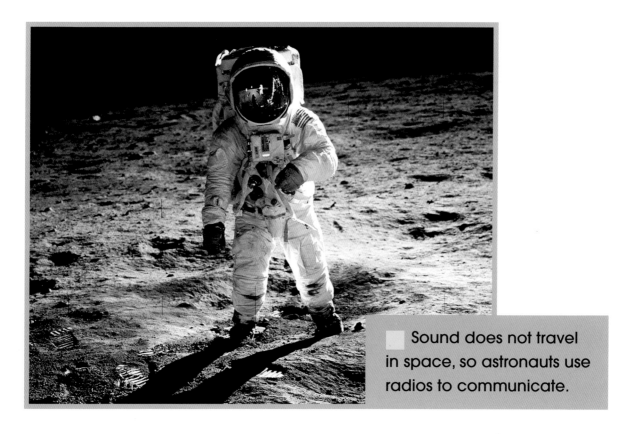

Sound does not travel in space, so astronauts use radios to communicate.

Fast and slow

Sound travels about four times faster through water than through air. Water molecules are close together so they pass vibrations on quickly. Underwater animals use sound to send messages to each other through the water.

Blue whales can communicate with other whales up to 850 km away.

Listen out!

You will need:
- 3 plastic sandwich bags
- water • sand • pencil

1 Fill the first bag 3/4 full with water. Fill the second bag 3/4 full with sand and blow air into about 3/4 of the third bag. Fasten securely.

2 Put the bags onto a table. Put your ear to each bag in turn, while you tap the table with a pencil.

3 Through which bag did you hear the tapping sound most clearly? Make a chart to record your findings.

Try filling additional bags with other materials, such as tissues or cooking oil. How do these materials affect the tapping sound?

Making sounds

You can make all kinds of different sounds by moving your body. You can use your voice to whisper, talk, sing and shout. You can clap your hands and stamp your feet.

Tapping and banging

Tapping and banging two objects together makes a sound. A door knocker bangs against the door. A drummer bangs a drum with drumsticks. A bell clapper hits the side of a bell to make it ring.

■ A woodpecker drums its beak against a tree, sending a loud, tapping sound through the forest.

■ Maracas are filled with beans or beads. They rattle when you shake them.

Shaking and rattling

Shaking moves small objects inside a container or rattles objects together to make a noise. A baby's rattle makes a noise when the baby shakes it. Maracas are rattles that are shaken in time to music.

Make a tambourine

You will need:
- 2 paper plates
- hole puncher
- buttons and beads
- coloured wool or ribbon
- pens or paints (or coloured paper and glue)
- foil, bottle tops or paper clips

1 Put the plates together and punch holes around the rims about 2 cm apart.

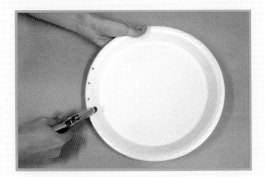

2 Separate the plates and put some buttons and beads on one plate.

3 Turn over the second plate. Put it over the first and line up the holes, so the bottom side of each plate is facing outwards. Thread the wool or ribbon through the holes and tie the ends so the plates are held closely together.

4 Colour the outer rim with pens or paints (or glue on some coloured shapes). You could also tie anything that jangles and rattles to the holes – bits of foil, bottle tops or paper clips.

Bang, rattle and shake your tambourine!

Hearing sounds

We have two ears, one on either side of our head. Our ears are the parts of our body we hear with. When sound waves travel into our ears, we hear the vibrations as a noise.

Ears

The part of our ears that we can see are called outer ears or ear flaps. They are shaped like a cup to catch sound waves. Our inner ears are the part of our ears we cannot see. They are made up of small, delicate parts.

If you cup your hand around your ear to make it bigger, you can hear quiet sounds more clearly.

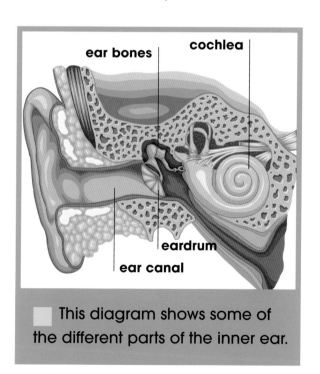

ear bones

cochlea

eardrum

ear canal

This diagram shows some of the different parts of the inner ear.

How our ears work

Sound waves travel along the **ear canal** and make the **eardrum** vibrate. Three tiny ear bones carry the vibrations to the **cochlea** which contains liquid. The vibrations travel through the liquid, then on to the brain as sound signals.

Make a model ear

Ask an adult to help you with this activity

You will need:
- foil tray (about 20 cm x 10 cm x 6 cm) • scissors • plastic food wrap • sticky tape
- bendy drinking straw • ping-pong ball • bowl of water

1 To make the eardrum, ask an adult to help you cut a hole in the base of the foil tray, about the size of the rim of a mug. Stretch the plastic wrap over the top of the foil tray and tape it in place.

2 For the ear bones, snip both ends of the drinking straw with scissors to make flaps. Tape the flaps of the bendy end of the straw to the ping-pong ball and tape the flaps of the other end of the straw to the middle of the plastic wrap.

3 The cochlea is the bowl of water. Rest the ping-pong ball on the surface of the water.

4 Speak through the hole in the base of the tray. Watch vibrations travel through all the parts of the ear and make ripples in the water.

Animal hearing

Some animals have very sharp hearing. They can hear a wider range of sounds than we can because they have specially **adapted** ears. They use their ears to find food or to escape from danger.

Hunters and hunted

Animals that are **predators**, such as foxes, and animals that are **prey**, such as rabbits, have big outer ears to collect the smallest sounds. Their ears can swivel to help them work out where the sound is coming from.

A predator points its ears towards its prey. It moves slowly and quietly so its prey does not hear it.

Bats have big ears to help them to hunt in the dark.

Amazing hearing

Bats hunt at night and use sound to catch moths for their food. They make very high squeaks and clicks. These sounds bounce off their prey and travel back as **echoes**. The echoes help the bat to work out where the moths are flying.

Make an ear trumpet

An ear trumpet is used as a hearing aid. It is shaped like a cone and helps to direct sounds into the ear.

You will need:
- sheet of A3 card • pencil
- string • scissors • sticky tape
- strip of card • pens or paints (or coloured paper and glue)

1 Draw a large semi-circle on the card and cut it out. To draw your semi-circle, mark half-way along the long edge of the card. Tie about 25 cm of string to a pencil. Hold down the end of the string with your finger on the mark. Pull the string tight and draw a semi-circle.

2 Roll the card into a cone shape, leaving a small opening at the narrow end. Tape the edges together.

3 Attach a strip of card to the underside of the cone to make a handle and decorate the cone with pens or paints (or glue on some coloured shapes).

4 Put the ear trumpet to your ear to hear quiet sounds louder. Speak through the cone and turn it into a **megaphone** to make your voice sound louder.

Near and far

The further away you are from a **sound source**, the quieter it sounds. The nearer you are, the louder it sounds. You can tell roughly how far away something is by how loud it sounds.

Thunder

When a thunderstorm is a few kilometres away, you see the flash of lightning seconds before you hear the crash of thunder. This is because sound travels at about 330 km per second – more slowly than light, which travels at about 300,000 km per second.

When a thunderstorm is overhead, you hear thunder and you see lightning at almost the same time.

Sound spreads out

At an airport, a passenger jet sounds very loud when it takes off! When the jet is high in the air, you can hardly hear it from the ground. This is because the sound waves have spread out and the sound is faint by the time it reaches your ears.

An airport worker wears earmuffs to protect her ears from the noisy jet.

Make a stethoscope

Ask an adult to help you with this activity

You will need:
- long cardboard tube
- 2 paper cups • sticky tape

1 Ask an adult to cut the narrow end off each of the paper cups.

2 Tape the narrow end of each cup to either end of the tube to make your stethoscope.

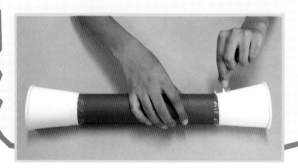

3 Put one end of the stethoscope onto your friend's chest, near to their heart. Put your ear to the other end of the stethoscope to listen to your friend's heart beat. How fast is the heart beating? What other faint sounds can you hear?

Doctors use stethoscopes to listen to sounds inside our body. A stethoscope makes quiet noises sound louder and nearer.

Bouncing sound

Sound bounces off surfaces like a ball bouncing off a wall. This is called **reflection**. Sounds bounce off hard, smooth surfaces in one direction. They bounce off rough surfaces in different directions.

Muffled!

When sounds hit a soft surface they are absorbed (or taken in). Noises can be **muffled** and made quieter with soft, absorbent material. Thick curtains in your bedroom help to muffle any outside sounds and give you a peaceful night's sleep.

The walls of a recording studio are lined with materials that absorb sound.

In an empty space like a cave, your voice will come back to you as an echo.

Echo

If you stand in a large, empty room and shout your name, you will hear it repeated back to you as an echo. The sound of your voice reflects off the walls back into your ears. You don't hear an echo in a small room full of furniture.

Make an echo catcher

You will need:
- chopping board • pile of books • 2 long cardboard tubes • coloured paper
- glue or sticky tape • pens or paints • sound source (such as a ticking clock or wind-up toy) • tea towel • sheet of corrugated cardboard

1 Use the books to prop up the chopping board on a table, to make a vertical 'wall'.

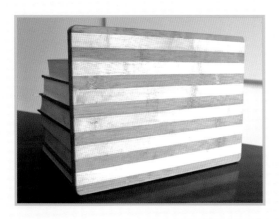

2 Wrap the cardboard tubes in coloured paper and decorate them. Lie the tubes on the table in a V-shape with the point of the V near to the chopping board.

3 Put the sound source at the end of one tube and your ear to the end of the other. You will hear the sound as it travels down one tube, reflects off the hard board and back along the other tube. What you hear is an echo.

4 Hang the tea towel over the chopping board and try again. Now replace the chopping board with the corrugated cardboard. Can you still hear the echo?

Musical sounds

Musicians in an orchestra pluck, scrape, blow, bang and rattle their instruments to make musical sounds. The **conductor** brings in the different instruments and shows the musicians how fast or slow to play.

Vibrating air

Musical sounds are caused by air vibrating around and inside an instrument. Air vibrates along the tube of a flute and inside a violin, for example. The shape, size and material the instrument is made from give it a particular sound.

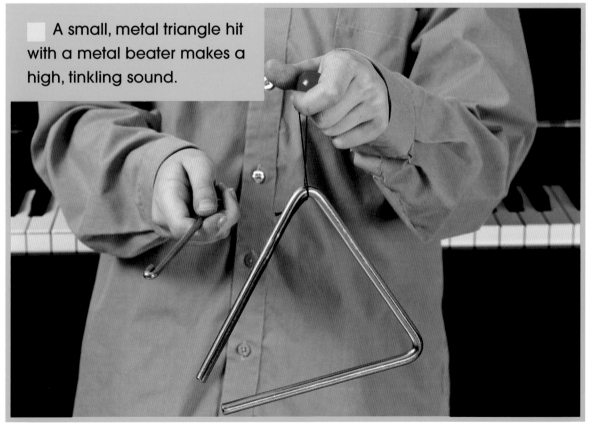

A small, metal triangle hit with a metal beater makes a high, tinkling sound.

Stringed instruments

Stringed instruments are plucked with fingers or scraped with a bow. The strings vibrate and air inside the instrument vibrates to make the sound louder. Thick strings vibrate slowly and make a low sound. Thin strings vibrate quickly and make a higher sound.

A violin has four strings. Each has a different thickness.

Make a stringed instrument

You will need:
- empty tissue box • pens (or glue and coloured paper)
- 3 long elastic bands of different widths • 2 pencils

1 Decorate your tissue box with pens or coloured paper. Stretch the elastic bands around the tissue box. Make sure they run over the hole.

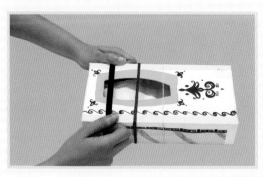

2 Push the pencils under the elastic bands at each side of the box. Pluck the bands between the pencils. Watch them vibrate and hear the different sounds they make.

3 Move the pencils towards the middle of the box to shorten the bands between the pencils, or towards the edges of the box to lengthen them. How can you make a very high or low sound?

Changing sounds

You can change musical sounds and make them higher and lower or louder and quieter. **Volume** is how loud or quiet a sound is. **Pitch** is how high or low a sound is.

Volume

Musicians make the sound of the instrument louder by blowing, scraping or hitting harder. They make the sound quieter by playing the instrument more gently. A loud sound makes big vibrations and a quiet sound makes smaller vibrations.

This musician uses beaters with padded ends to make a soft, quiet sound. When he hits the drum harder, the sound gets louder.

Pitch

The pitch of a **note** changes when its vibrations become faster or slower. Players play different notes by changing the length of the string (or tube of air) of their instruments.

A piccolo (left) plays high notes and a bass flute (right) plays low notes. Pressing the keys makes the tube of air slightly longer or shorter.

Make a tuned wind instrument

You will need:
- plastic bottles of different sizes
- large jug of water coloured with food colouring • pencil

1 Pour some water into one of the bottles. Practise blowing across the open bottle top to make the air inside it vibrate and play a note. Alternatively, tap the bottle lightly with a pencil.

2 Experiment with the amount of water and size of the bottle to play notes of different pitches.

3 Arrange the bottles in order from low notes on the left to the highest note on the right.

You now have a tuned wind instrument!

Ultrasound

Sound that is too high for us to hear is called **ultrasound**. Even though we can't hear ultrasound, we can use it in all kinds of different ways.

Sound pictures

Ultrasound is used to make pictures of things that we wouldn't normally be able to see, such as an unborn baby or a shipwreck on the bottom of the ocean. Ultrasound waves are sent out and reflected off the object. These echoes are shown as a picture on a screen.

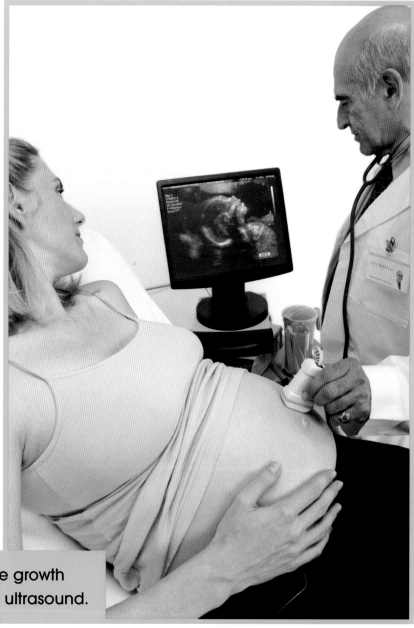

Doctors can check the growth of an unborn baby using ultrasound.

Cleaning

Ultrasound can be used for cleaning. Ultrasound waves vibrate a mixture of water and cleaning solution to remove dirt without causing damage. Ultrasound is used in some toothbrushes or to clean small, delicate objects such as jewellery.

An ultrasonic toothbrush vibrates the fluid in your mouth to help remove food and bacteria.

Silent whistles

Dogs can hear much higher sounds than we can. A dog will prick up its ears to hear a sound that we can't hear at all. Dog owners use silent whistles with a very high note to give their dog orders that only they can hear.

Dogs have very sensitive hearing. They can be trained using a high-pitched whistle.

Glossary

adapted

A plant or animal that has adapted has changed (over millions of years) to suit its surroundings.

cochlea

The cochlea is part of the inner ear shaped like a snail shell. Sound waves pass through fluid in the cochlea.

communicate

When people and animals communicate, they give each other information by speaking, making sounds or sending signals.

conductor

A conductor is the person in charge of an orchestra. The conductor signals when to play loudly or quietly, faster or slower.

ear canal

The ear canal is found just behind the ear flap. Sound waves pass along this tunnel to the inner ear.

eardrum

The eardrum is at the end of the ear canal. It is a piece of skin that vibrates like a drum when sound waves hit it.

echo

An echo happens when sound waves bounce back at you off a hard surface and you hear the same sound twice.

gas

Gases are materials that have no shape. They spread out because the molecules are not held together.

liquid

A liquid is a material that flows and pours because the molecules are held loosely together.

megaphone

A megaphone is a device shaped like a cone that makes your voice sound louder.

molecules

A molecule is a very small part. Solids, liquids and gases are made up of billions of tiny molecules.

muffled

Sound is muffled when it is made quieter.

note

A note is a sound of a particular pitch, either sung or played on a musical instrument.

pitch

The pitch of a note is how high or low it sounds.

predators

Animals that are predators hunt other animals for food.

prey

Animals that are prey are hunted by other animals for food.

reflection

Reflection happens when sound bounces off a hard surface.

solid

A solid is a material that can hold its shape because the molecules are packed closely together.

sound source

A sound source makes a sound.

sound waves

Sound travels through the air in sound waves. Sound waves are made when air vibrates.

ultrasound

Ultrasonic sound (ultrasound) is too high for us to hear.

vibrations

Vibrations are very small, fast movements to and fro.

vocal cords

Your vocal cords are in your throat. They vibrate and produce sounds when air passes through them.

volume

The volume of a sound is how loud or quiet it is.

Index